W9-AAF-662

A FORTRESS BOOK

EVERYMAN A PRIEST

by

Karl H. Hertz

MUHLENBERG PRESS • PHILADELPHIA

Library of Congress Catalog Card Number 61-6754

Printed in U.S.A. UB2006

FOREWORD

The need for putting what we, as Christians, believe into words everybody can readily understand poses a constant challenge. In response to that challenge the New Testament itself was written in a language commonly spoken and understood. Through the ages handbooks, catechisms, and tracts have been written and, since the invention of printing, published to meet the need for clarifying in every age what it means to be a Christian.

Whether it is more difficult to be a Christian in one age than another is hard to say. But being a Christian in the second half of the twentieth century is becoming more and more complicated. This heightens the challenge of spelling out for our day in an uncomplicated way what it means to be a Christian. To put the thought patterns of theology into terms that are readily understood is not easy. Yet saying what we believe in such a way that others, without too much difficulty, will understand what we are talking about is the test of our own grasp of what we believe and hold to be true.

In tackling this task the authors of Fortress Books do not try to make a difficult faith seem easy but to make it easier for the reader to see how demanding Christian discipleship really is and how important it is for him to give meaning to what he believes in what he does. And so the authors want to give the reader clues to guide him in making his decisions from day to day. It is the hope of the publishers that these small books, dealing with central themes of Christian faith and life, may succeed in their purpose.

Helmut T. Lehmann
Editor

CONTENTS

WHAT IT MEANS TO BE A CHRISTIAN

During this past winter my daughter attended a concert with the rest of the family. Very carefully she noted each item on the program as it was played. At the end, in response to the demands of the audience, the artist played an encore. Baffled by the fact that she could find nothing on the program, my daughter turned to me for an explanation. "It's an extra piece," I told her. Quickly she came back with the question, "Is it allowed?"

Some such question may in all likelihood have bothered many Christians during the years of the Reformation when Martin Luther announced that all Christians were priests. Could this be true? Were lay people now to hear confession, say mass, and pronounce absolution? Or did the good doctor from Wittenberg have something else in mind?

Probably first-century Christians asked similar questions, especially when they read the letters from Paul of Tarsus. For example, at Colossae, when Paul wrote to the faithful there, "In view of these tremendous facts, don't let anyone worry you by criticizing what you eat or drink, or what holy days you ought to observe, or bothering you over new moons or Sabbaths. All these things have at most only a symbolical value; the solid fact is Christ." Was all this really possible? Could one break the cake of inherited religious custom this freely?

Surely a man would not escape unscathed if he violated what men had for centuries accepted as the duties of a consecrated piety. We are so familiar (perhaps not by knowledge of Scripture but as the result of generations of Protestant freedom) with some of these liberties from the ancient religious prescriptions that we fail to grasp what a sharp and radical word Paul had spoken. The sharpness of the whole debate over circumcision, even in those few records that are preserved, as well as Paul's frequent return to certain themes, ought to remind us that long-established ways of doing things were being challenged and overthrown.

REPRESENTATIVES OF THE NEW HUMANITY

By the same token we do not really grasp the radical import of what Paul had to say about the Christian life. Like coins worn smooth from long usage, we pass these words from one to another, seldom stopping to scrutinize the texts for the prophetic implications that are in them. "God's picked representatives of the new humanity," Paul calls Christian people. He urges them "to live life with a due sense of responsibility, as those who know the meaning of life." Like my seven-year-old daughter we may well ask, "Is it really allowed?"

We are as Christians, moreover, the victims of the tides of human history. In our day the streams of events have been running in strange ways. Sometimes, in fact, we act like those whom the storms have shipwrecked on some lonely and obscure island. The landscape changes before our eyes into an increasingly strange, unfamiliar, and threatening terrain. What were familiar landmarks turn out to be, as we check such charts as we have salvaged, quite different from what our senses told us. Or rather, the very markings on the charts change before our eyes.

In such circumstances we may ask not only what it means to be a priest, but also what it means to be a Christian; even, in fact, what it means to be a man. What, if anything, is really allowed? Or possible? And if we consult those who have been shipwrecked with us, we find that in various ways these questions are the fashionable topics of all conversations.

Meanwhile, to continue the figure of speech for a moment, we walk along the seashore to see what the rising tide is washing in to us. Will there be some message from beyond? some ultimate word? some container with a cosmic formula of hope which a mysterious Merlin has somewhere cast upon the waters for us to find? What indeed might not the human mind anticipate when the reported realities of the front pages are often as fantastic as the creations of the untrammeled imagination of the wildest artistic spirit?

The tide indeed washes up many things, salvage and debris, broken pieces of nature's handiwork and man's craftsmanship. And it washes them away again, to return at its next appointed interval with wet cargo bartered from the deep. Yet what it brings is fragmentary, transient, rarely yielding more than a clue to help the man on shore piece together the answers.

Such tides seem continually to run in the affairs of men. For from one interval of time to the next fragments of insight are swept ashore, tempting the beachcomber to gather the pieces and take them home, where he might puzzle out from them the larger drift of events. Sometimes the seas run high and strong, as the storms of change batter the landscape into another shape. Sometimes, as in our day apparently, they run in surges of piety on one side of the sphere and surges of impiety upon the other.

There are those for whom the image of the tides tells the whole story. For the tide will turn again, and after the turbulence and the noise of the breaking waters, nothing will be left but a beach scoured clean—bright and gleaming and empty. And so the fashions of thought and action ebb and flow with occasional salvage and debris left behind, occasionally a bottle with an indecipherable message, but all of it carrying no meaning beyond the monotonous routine of the waters coming and going.

WHO AM I?

These are images of despair and disillusionment, hardly calculated to answer man's recurring question, "Who am I?" But it will not do to ignore them, for if the images of man in our day sometimes appear to us as portraits hung in a madhouse, we must not forget that in each of the grotesque likenesses we are asked to see some reflection of ourselves. If, over against them, we finally claim that a different image is the authentic one, it may be that we shall only uncover it by scraping off the overlay of caricature to get to the original work.

There is, of course, another approach. The words which St. Paul wrote to the churches of the Mediterranean world centuries ago, the magnificent vision of the Christian life which Luther had, also spoke to this condition. Paul and Luther, Calvin and some of the other reformers were not unmindful of the turbulence and uproar of their day. In fact, it was to just this kind of situation that they addressed themselves. They spoke to men in the midst of world-sweeping changes—changes perhaps not as rapid or as apparent in centuries without daily news broadcasts, statistical indicators, and a persistent preoccupation with the latest novelties.

But there were changes—tremendous changes. The sweep of Christianity across the Roman world with its Gospel of the cross was itself the most revolutionary event of the restless first century. The sweep of the Reformation across the world of Western Europe was part of an equally revolutionary epoch. In both instances the bold announcement of a new image of man, a new doctrine of man, played a major part in transforming human existence and the social order.

But in our day the tides of change are apparently running in the opposite direction. The Gospel is hardly sweeping the world. The doctrines of man which are fashionable more frequently suggest that he is a purposeless anachronism in the vast impersonal currents of global change and cosmic process. The odds would almost seem to be that the Gospel is more likely to be swept up and deposited in the dustbin of history.

Still, it may very well be that the renewed interest in the doctrine of the calling and of the universal priesthood may have an important role to play in a Christian answer to the confusions and contradictions of our time. It may even be, as I firmly believe, that much of the apparent irrelevance of the activities of church members arises from a perversion of the doctrine of the universal priesthood and a retreat from the kinds of responsibilities which Christians should be assuming. We have something more important to do than to take refuge from the storms; we are called to full, active, and courageous participation in the affairs of the world.

WHAT IT MEANS TO BE A CHRISTIAN

But the Christian man must know who he is if he is to live his life with a due sense of responsibility. "Don't send a boy when you need a man," was a characteristic jeer of the enlisted men of the United States Army when some inept and unqualified person was put in charge of a difficult duty. St. Paul threw out the same challenge to the Christians of Corinth centuries ago, "When I was a little child I talked and felt and thought like a little child. Now that I am a man my childish speech and feeling and thought have no further significance for me."

How then do we define a Christian? What does it mean to say, "I am a Christian"?

The answer is deceptively simple—and humanly impossible. For a Christian is not defined by what he is; he is defined by what he ought to be. Better still, he is defined by what God has made him and intended him to be, however imperfect the performance, however poorly the reality fulfils the promise.

God has made me a Christian. Whenever I identify myself properly, I identify myself as God's man, his handiwork through the redemptive deed of Christ.

If to be a Christian is to be what God intends me to be, then the attempt to describe the nature of this kind of man must have a radical point of departure. I must seek out in man what is reflected back from an Eternal original, to see what is there—not indeed in the pristine creature into whom God once breathed the breath of life, but rather disclosing what happened and could happen when the lost, defeated, and restless vagabond discovered that new life comes with death. This is a portrayal of *the second man* whom God made, after the image of the Son himself. This is an exposition of the most incredible possibility of all, that the original after whom I am shaped is none other than the Holy One himself, that the prodigal is by the miracle of grace none other than a son of the Most High God—redeemed and restored to the image of God himself. This is my new being: to be one of those whom the apostle called "the picked representatives of the new humanity."

No logic can demonstrate the authenticity of the Christian man, for this humanity rests on a divine deed of restoration. Being a Christian is the result of an encounter, after which I cannot be the same, though outwardly I remain the same man; it is a figure fashioned of faith, nurtured by grace, living by hope. In the face of all the evidence of continuing human failure, we must nevertheless attempt to live this life, and in the living of it lies the only possible critique and reply to the portraits hung in the madhouse of this generation. We must therefore attempt to set down the major dimensions of the life of the new man, the Christian man. The lines which define these dimensions all take their beginning from the Son himself, for it is only as his brothers that we can discern the qualities of our own roles.

Thus, as the Son appears to us in those glimpses we

catch of him in the Gospel as priest, king, and prophet, so we are also called to similar roles. All of us are priests, kings, and prophets: priests called to handle the sacred things of the creation with reverent care; kings endowed with authority to be used in responsible service; prophets driven to protest every betrayal with radical dissent.

Priest, king, and prophet—this is what I am meant to be. This is what I will be and cannot escape being. Yet each of these, I will discover, has its own perversions and temptations. Each of them after my own fashion I can twist into a caricature of my second humanity, making of them evil and demonic things. I undertake this examination of my destiny fully aware that what I am to be is something that God gives, yet once the gift is in my hands I may misuse it, like a vagabond scavenging the rubbish heaps of the world in a cast-off dress suit, a prodigal run off from the father a second time and inevitably headed for the darkest corner of Skid Row.

Be that as it may. This little book simply wants to make it clear what it means to be a particular kind of man—a Christian man. Though it will not ignore what man has done and learned, its point of departure will be what God has given. For the skeptic let this description be offered simply as an hypothesis, or better still as a kind of challenge, another picture hung in the exhibition hall of mankind. Let him examine it in comparison with the others. It only makes the claim that this image of man provides a meaningful way of dealing with all that he may encounter in his existence.

To understand the image, however, we must look at it in all its details. We must examine in turn what it means to be a priest, a king, and a prophet.

THE CHRISTIAN AS PRIEST IN PRAYER AND ACTION

The elevation of Mr. Ezra Taft Benson to the post of Secretary of Agriculture in the Eisenhower cabinet made Americans conscious not only of the strength of the Church of Jesus Christ of the Latter Day Saints but also of a particular brand of lay piety. For in Mormonism every man is a priest, not only in the vague sense in which American Protestants often speak of the universal priesthood of believers but also in a very specific way. Mormons have two orders of priesthood; depending upon qualifications, each Mormon male is ordained first into a lower order of the priesthood of Aaron, then into successively higher orders and, if he meets the required conditions, into the priesthood of Melchizedek, once more in terms of specific ordination and responsibility.

A PRIEST IS NOT AN AMATEUR "HOLY MAN"

The Mormon priesthoods illustrate both the immense power of the Protestant doctrine of the universal priesthood and its characteristic perversion, not only among Mormons but also among Protestants generally. For its usual expression in Protestantism has been in terms of lay religious duties; in extreme Protestant groups in terms of a radical insistence on a lay "ministry" (that is, without specific professional training, usually unpaid). To be a priest is to be a kind of an amateur "holy man," a religious virtuoso. Like all gifted amateurism this lay priesthood achieves its success by diligent attention to a narrow range of skills, in this instance specifically religious skills. Thus "the lay priest" is really an amateur clergyman. In fact, this is often taken to be the real aim of genuine piety among the laity, with the not infrequent consequence that when a layman begins to take religion "seriously" people expect him to become a minister.

Obviously, if the universal priesthood were this kind of affair, only two alternatives would be open. First, only a few could really fulfil the meaning of the universal priesthood in their lives. Amateurism, especially in America, is a time-consuming affair, requiring hours of concentrated practice and regular performance, as any observer of amateur athletics, golf and tennis for example, can observe. To be this kind of amateur means either to have means of one's own, so that one can devote the time to learning the skills or, as any follower of athletics can tell you, to receive compensation "under the table," expense allowances, special prizes, and so forth. The real amateurs of American athletics are the backyard dubs. If belonging to the universal priesthood means to be an amateur "holy man," only the select few will ever attain this standing.

The second possibility is that we recognize degrees of priesthood in the manner of the Mormons in order to take care of the differing circumstances, aptitudes, abilities, and available time of different persons. In a sense, we give the real amateurs a kind of "religious handicap score," such as the local golf club uses to entice the dubs into its annual membership tournament. Naturally the dubs never win, but they can console themselves with the fact that, counting their handicap, they gave the club champion a real struggle. In effect, at the upper levels no difference exists, except in name, between the gifted amateur and the professional, between the "lay priest" and the clergyman. All the differences are now differences in degree, and the poor performer can always be told that if he would only devote more time to religious activities, he would become a better man.

Herein lies the misinterpretation, for the difference between layman and clergyman is not one of degree of religious activity (or of "holiness" for that matter) but one of office. No special virtue or quantitative advantage in righteousness attaches to the one or to the other. The universal priesthood applies to the clergyman as well as to the layman. The doctrine denies the existence of orders or degrees within the church. It rejects outright the notion of a select few as the virtuosi of Christianity, whether amateur or professional. Within the universal priesthood differences of office exist, but no differences in degree of religiosity.

This is why we must reject the persistent temptation to suggest that the really consecrated layman ought to become a clergyman. Far from it. While we ought not disparage the office of the clergy, we must recognize that there is a genuine lay priesthood in life and in worship.

Perhaps at this point it is best to examine what the word "priest" means. A priest in the practice of all religions is one who handles sacred things and shows in his handling of them that these things reveal the relationship between man and God. This description covers the native medicine man who uses, for example, the skull of an ancestor to evoke the action of a spirit, and the Christian minister officiating at an altar. Seen from the outside, they are both handling sacred things (sacred by the definition of the devotee) and showing forth a relationship to the divine or Holy One. A Christian, to be specific, is a priest whenever and wherever he handles the things of this world with reverent care and awareness of the fact that God has made them. In so doing, he recognizes a "sacred" quality in them and at the same time proclaims for himself and to his neighbors a connection between the Creation and the Creator.

Secondly, a priest is one who approaches God on behalf of others. The universal priesthood denies, as it must, that there is a special order of persons appointed as mediators between God and man. Every man stands before God alone. Yet, in a sense which we shall distinguish from mediation, every man may also stand before God on behalf of others. This does not mean, however, that every man carries on the same kind of religious activities.

What a priest does offers the clue to understanding what the universal priesthood is. I have defined him as one who handles the things of this world with an awareness of the fact that they are sacred and that in handling them he is revealing the relationship between man and God, creature and Creator. This is probably unfamiliar language to most men. The same action can, however, be described by saying that the Christian lives the life of faith at all times, not just in church on Sunday morning. Or we could say that employment in a "secular" calling may for the Christian be work in a vocation to which God has called him. These assertions show the interconnectedness of basic Protestant ideas. Still the emphasis on priesthood will illuminate aspects of the "life of faith" from a different perspective than "calling" affords.

A PRIEST HANDLES SACRED THINGS

The first clue is in the notion of "reverent care for the creation." This notion is almost impossible to illustrate from contemporary American life, for we have been deeply secularized, and our handling of the things of this world has been perverted. To begin, we may specify what reverent care cannot mean. It must exclude sheer exploitation of the world for our own good. It must also exclude, perhaps not as obviously to some, enlightened self-interest. (I have never been able to understand what is "enlightened" about this kind of self-interest; it seems to suggest simply a more subtle and sophisticated cunning in the arts of acquisition.) The farmer who cares for the soil because this is the way to a better crop and to higher profits is indeed, in human terms, a better farmer. But he is not necessarily a priest, for his attitude toward the creation is still essentially utilitarian, not reverent. Similarly, the man who participates in programs for the community good because he finds co-operation a more efficient way of doing things and feels that "everyone ought to do his part" is still operating within a framework that is outside the Gospel.

Reverent care is man's awareness of dealing with something that is given to him, something that he has not made. He knows he lives in a created world, a world in which all things are sustained at every moment by the providential love and majestic sovereign power of the Creator. "The heavens are telling the glory of God, and the firmament proclaims his handiwork," and so does the automobile a man drives and the barbecue pit he constructs in his backyard. All things are a part of God's world. Furthermore, this statement also holds true for the patient in the physician's office and the student in the classroom, as well as for the roast in the oven and the machine on the assembly line. Because these things are given to us, directly or indirectly, our first obligation is to care for them. Care may, of course, include use; but care comes first.

At the heart of the priestly response is clear and confident acceptance of God as the Creator. "I believe that God has created me and all that exists," that he has given me many kinds of good things as a part of the manifold diversity of his creation, even the very ordinary things of life such as "clothing and shoes, house and home." As a Christian I accept what God gives me as good; not perfect indeed, for I know the corruption with which all things have been infected, but nevertheless still bearing the marks of the benevolence of the Maker. To be a priest is to know the world as given, not just in some impersonal and accidental way, but as given into my care personally, within the range of my activities, as a gift of unlimited love.

The priestly attitude toward the world is, therefore, an entirely different attitude from the attitude which sees the world simply as something made for man's use. Nature is not just a stage where we may shift the scenery as we please; it is God's handiwork and the place where he acts. I may indeed delight in the plenitude of the Creator, in the outpouring of the riches of God's goodness by which he cares for his people. And I may use nature for myself and for others, if I understand it fully as God has given it, as a creation.

To this notion of the priesthood we can attach two words that will spell out its meaning very concretely. What a priest does with the objects he handles shows that these objects are in some sense sacred. But there is no special category of sacred things in the world. What is sacred has no special color or design or weight or composition; no neon lights flash on and off; no flaming arrows point; no electric shock jars the unaware. The sacred may be stone or wood, mountain or tree, water, bread, or wine. But because it is handled in a particular way to show forth "the holy" it is sacred in a particular context. To be sacred is "to make something holy manifest." (The Greek word for this is *hierophany.*) Even more specifically, as can be seen from the Christian sacraments, to be sacred is "to make God manifest." (*Theophany.*) Luther's explanation of the use of water in baptism is very clear on this point. "Water by itself cannot work any such great miracle; it is the Word of God that is in and with the water."

When the way an object is handled makes that object a source of "revelation," the object is "a sacred object." This way of handling an object, as the scientific study of religion shows, most frequently is embedded in the rituals used by the professional holy men of a group. (Our point here is, of course, that the priesthood is not thus limited.) What these men do in their rites of sacrifice and propitiation is usually either the imitation of some original divine action or obedience to a divine command. Thus the celebration of the New Year among many societies is a re-enactment of the creation of the world. All things are once again made new. Actually, in the astronomical sense, no one day is more adapted to the beginning of the year than another. It is the ritual observance that makes the day holy. It makes it a day of rebirth and renewal, and it does so by imitating the original divine action. Even in our society remnants of this practice remain. The New Year's Eve orgy is a kind of admission of the setting in of chaos as the old order goes out, symbolized by a doddering old man; New Year's Day is marked by resolutions, a new beginning, and by the symbol of a newborn infant.

This provides us then with a fuller description of what the word "priest" means. I can handle the things of this earth as profane things, that is for what they are simply as objects (just as one day is like another) and for what I can get out of them. Or I can by my handling of them let their holiness shine through, making God manifest, by reverent care, by awareness of the depth and height of the relationships in which all things stand.

A PRIEST APPROACHES GOD ON BEHALF OF OTHERS

To be a priest is not only to be a man who stands before God in a certain way but also one who stands before God on behalf of others, for a priest is never a priest for himself alone. Many of the excesses of Protestant individualism in the church and elsewhere would have been avoided if we had retained our consciousness that while each man does stand directly before God without human mediation, he also stands before God on behalf of his neighbor. To make clear that this relationship on behalf of others is not one of mediation, that is one in which I secure the grace of God for someone else by my action (for this I cannot do and need not do), we shall call this priestly action *intercession.* The choice of the word is deliberate; it refers generally to prayer or to a request to God on behalf of someone in need. Intercessory action is priestly action; it includes much more than formal prayer. In fact, as we shall see, unless ordinarily it goes beyond formal prayer it is ritualism, the characteristic priestly vice, and not Christian intercession at all.

Basically the argument is simply that the Gospel did not set me free from the bondage of sin in order that I might hereafter be preoccupied with my own piety and righteousness. Quite the contrary. It directs my activity toward others.

Thus I see in every other creature of God someone for whom I am to care. This is, of course, distressingly abstract. But it can be startlingly particular. The man in need, the man farthest down, is the man whom Jesus defines as my neighbor, who needs my "practical sympathy," my practice of sympathy. Here too is something which God gives. That he has put me in this particular place in life, in relationship to this particular person who requires just the kind of help that I can give (even though I may not always recognize this)—this is to be one of God's priests, one who handles what God has given with reverent care. More generally, I must care for the hurt and unwanted, the demoralized and the lost, for God has set me to be his agent. "I was in prison and you visited me." He has not told me how, but he has put the riches of his world at my disposal. I see myself in a new role as the priest through whom what God gives is made available to the stranger in need.

THE CHRISTIAN: A PRIEST IN PRAYER AND ACTION

To see what priestly action means in its fullest sense requires an analysis of intercessory action.

Intercessory action begins with prayer; all too often it ends there. To pray without ceasing is a piece of hyperbolic advice appropriate for an apostle. His life was one of intercessory action, supported by its constant relationship to God. But when prayer is reduced to an exercise of the tongue, to a kind of ritualistic babbling of holy words that remain uncomplemented by holy deeds, one may question whether the advice applies.

The temptation to include everything under one aspect of the Christian life of faith is always present in the church. If there were a Department of Prayer (God forbid!) no doubt the Pauline admonition could be cited as proof that all of the Christian life is prayer, just as some would insist that all of it is worship, stewardship, evangelism, social action, or what have you.

Still there is a fundamental truth in the emphasis on prayer. Intercessory prayer is the model for intercessory action. For when we intercede in prayer for the neighbor in want, the nation in turmoil, the community under disaster, the test of the validity of the intercession is quite simple. For if I pray that God may restore what has been broken in the life of my neighbor, nation, or community and fervently hope that God will answer my prayer, then I must run the risk that the answer will be, "All right, your neighbor is in trouble. You know about it; now go help him." Intercessory prayer is a prayer spoken with the hope of intercessory action. Sometimes, I suspect, it is the hope that someone else will do the necessary dirty work; it is a technique for evading responsibility. But unless I am ready and willing to accept the possibility that the necessary action must be my action, that God may direct me to seize the opportunity because I occupy a place where my neighbor's need is apparent to me, I am reducing intercession to an act of blasphemy. If my prayer is just a pious way of saying, "Let George do it," I hardly need pray at all.

As priest I must act on behalf of my neighbor who is in need. My neighbor is one in whom I must see the Lord, "hungry, naked, imprisoned, sick" and be called into action. What is important here is what I do to serve my neighbor's needs, not whether I use pious words. I need not even see that what I am doing is a religious act. But the heart of the Christian priesthood is just this intercessory action on behalf of others.

Thus the doctor who uses his gifts to heal the diseases of the body, the social worker whose insight and understanding help restore a broken relationship, and the school teacher who skilfully stimulates the mind of a child to productive learning—all of these are priests.

Even when they don't know it. For the care of the creation and of mankind is not the exclusive prerogative of Christians. God in his providence not only lets his rain fall on just and on the unjust alike, but he also uses the purely human qualities of sympathy and concern for others to achieve his ends. This is sometimes hard for Christians to understand. In fact, more than one Christian theologian has disparaged the virtues of the unbelievers as if they were vices. More than one Christian evidently believes that unless an explicit label is pinned on the action, unless the sacred musicians announce the work of the priests with a flourish on their trumpets, the action is not good, certainly not a priestly action.

This is a strange doctrine, largely the illegitimate offspring of a wrong-headed application of the doctrine of original sin. But why should we disparage and condemn actions that contribute to the welfare of our neighbors when non-Christians perform these actions? True, they are not actions that earn salvation; but then, neither are ours. Let us rather thank God that in this world the performance of deeds of compassion and justice is not limited to Christians. The plenitude of the grace of God is such that he can and does use all men to achieve his providential goals.

A difference does exist. More so than others, Christians recognize the full meaning and scope of intercessory action. For to intercede for others belongs to the essence of the Christian life flowing from the "new being in Christ." Furthermore, Christian intercession knows no limits. Neither the condition of my neighbor, his moral standards, the disorganized nature of his existence, not even his ingratitude can justify refusal of my help. He need not be my kinsman, fellow-countryman, or fellow-believer. He need only be a human being who requires what I am in a position to offer. My help is not offered conditionally, depending on whether he deserves it, any more than God's gift of grace is offered to me conditionally, depending on whether I deserve it.

Christian intercession is unlimited in another way. For I dare not count the cost or the gain to myself, even if it involves giving my life for another. This action is, of course, the ultimate measure of intercession. Only infrequently would most of us have the strength to go this far—in scriptural language "to go the second mile" all the way. For in these circumstances we realize the full import of what Jesus meant when he said that "he who loses his life for my sake shall gain it." Here too we recognize that only as we have fully encountered Christ as Lord and learned to trust him completely is this sacrifice possible.

A NEW DIMENSION: THE GOSPEL

At this point, above all, the Christian as priest knows that he must be supported and nourished by the gift of grace. When he goes the second mile, beyond what our usual standards of justice require, he knows the truth of St. Paul's magnificent words, "Not that we are sufficient of ourselves to do anything as of ourselves, but our sufficiency is of Christ."

Another dimension of intercessory action is uniquely Christian. For ordinary fairness is essentially a matter of principles, of a code of ethics, of law. It is part of the radical transformation of the law which the Gospel brings about that men see that at every point justice must be joined with love. What is required is transformed by compassion. For to be a Christian is to be free from the pressures of a moral code. Works follow from faith, but they are not a condition of faith. As such they are the acts of free men on behalf of others, not just obedience to rules of conduct. The Gospel requires that the law be used constructively, creatively, compassionately on behalf of all.

The police officer may serve as an illustration. Only rarely would any of us think of the performance of his duties as a priestly act. Yet to work constructively in the maintenance of order requires more than a literal enforcement of legal rules. The Christian as a police officer handles the law; this is his duty. But it is the law in a Christian perspective. The fullest performance of his duty lies not so much in the apprehension of the wrong-doer (necessary as such action is) but in an enforcement of law which protects the well-being of others, inspires them to obedience, and whenever possible (particularly in dealing with certain kinds of offenders) in such constructive use of his authority as will serve to salvage and restore the violator. Such police officers exist—especially on the juvenile squads of some communities—officers who would rather help the wrong-doer "go straight," who would rather make their office a positive and constructive force in the community than a punitive and threatening one. The tragedy is that Christians have often paid little attention to these possibilities. They do not see that such a man can truly engage in intercessory action on behalf of a neighbor. Here is a real opportunity for the exercise of the priesthood of believers.

In the same way we can point to the constructive, intercessory action possible for businessmen in the performance of their work. I am not thinking now of charitable activities (United Funds, and so forth); I am thinking of the businessman who institutes personnel policies which without paternalism, without mere profit-seeking utilitarian designs, help his employees to a better sense of their dignity as persons and their responsibilities as producers. I am thinking too of the intercessory action possible for the realtor. A thousand cities are calling for adequate housing for their poorly paid inhabitants, for decent and inexpensive housing without the segregation of the ghetto for Negroes. Here is a genuine opportunity —no man is in a better position to do these things than the man whose daily occupation is in these affairs. God may indeed have appointed him to this place. Naturally it will not be easy. Who said it was supposed to be? We need not assume that businessmen, especially Christian businessmen, are always looking for the easiest way to do things.

REAL WORSHIP

But how in the world is all of this related to worship, traditionally the main occupation of priests? The answer is not difficult and, once stated, it ought to be obvious to the Christian.

Worship as an independent activity of the religious person, separated in kind and in meaning from his daily existence, is a travesty of divine action. In fact, those who worship in this manner are polytheists, paying homage to one god on Sunday (what god it is difficult to say, since he cannot be the Maker of heaven *and earth*) and other gods on weekdays. Nor will it do simply to utter a few pious but irrelevant prayers each morning and evening, the words of which are totally unrelated to the day's activities. Or, more subtly still, to think that one is a Christian at one's work because one engaged in a conversation about religion—when perhaps one ought to be concerned about the need of one's neighbor at that particular moment. (We may, of course, talk about religion; the point here is that priestly action—reverent handling of what God gives and intercessory action on behalf of others—is not limited to pious words or biblical topics of conversation.)

Each of these illustrations indicates the peculiar and probably widespread perversion of the universal priesthood. By restricting priestly action to obvious religious acts (singing hymns, saying prayers, and reading the Bible) we may in fact be denying that God created the world. The division of life into sacred and secular areas is false. To say that dimensions of life exist in which I cannot act as a priest is to deny that these dimensions are under the sovereignty of God. Yet this is exactly what we do time and time again—when, for example, we think that the religiously concerned layman ought to become a minister, or when we think that the proper technique for "getting religion into industry" is to hold prayer meetings in factories rather than to solve the difficult problems of labor-management relationships.

In general, the temptation we face is to reduce the universal priesthood to an ecclesiastical function, to particularize the universal, dressing ourselves up in liturgical vestments and rehearsing a few properly devout phrases. The universal priesthood is universal. It includes all men in all the activities of life.

Yet worship does have a place of first importance. For this is where I begin and this is the place to which I constantly return. In worship I participate in the explicit and dramatically enacted (liturgy) assertion of God's total claim upon my life. From worshiping I gain my perspective, here is the center from which the lines of influence reach out even to the farthest and most hidden corners of human existence. God's total claim is what worship proclaims in word and deed.

Worship is also where I am constantly renewed. To be a priest is to live in a continuing relationship to God. My life as a priest needs nourishment, refreshment, instruction. To make worship such an experience is a part of the task of the church, particularly of the ministry, which must proclaim the Word with sufficient clarity and scope that each man can recognize and accept the priestly role into which God has placed him and gain ever-renewed strength for its performance.

All of us are priests, whether we want to be or not. We may be apostate, ignorant, heretical, or rebellious. But we cannot help handling sacred things and we are bound to our fellowmen, even if we belong among that number which has never heard the Gospel. But the Christian is a priest consciously, in full awareness of his responsibilities before God and to his fellowmen. To him we may apply the admonition of St. Paul that he must "live life with a due sense of responsibility, not as an ignorant person, but as one who knows the meaning of life."

THE CHRISTIAN AS KING IN RESPONSIBLE SERVICE

All men are featherless bipeds.

Plucked hens are featherless bipeds.

Therefore, all men are plucked hens.

A professor of formal logic could quickly point out several technical errors in this chain of thought, but I am sure that no one except other professors of formal logic and their captive student audiences would bother to listen. Even the proverbial village half-wit senses that "it just ain't so."

THE PURPOSE OF LIFE

Common sense tells us that man is different from the barnyard fowl, from the beasts of the field, even from his biological near-relatives, the anthropoid apes. I want to look at just one way of spelling out this difference. Man is the only creature for whom events have significance. To put it crudely, not even the finest horses bred in Kentucky would ever have invented the Kentucky Derby; as far as I know, no TV announcer has ever interviewed the winning horse.[1]

Men do remember their accomplishments. By monuments and written chronicles, in epic verse and anniver-

[1] We have to be careful in making assertions of this kind; nothing is apparently impossible in television.

sary celebration, they set down the records of their deeds —sometimes with considerable boasting.

Man is more than what he eats or drinks. In fact, his eating and drinking are as often matters of ceremony as they are of hunger and thirst. Wedding breakfasts, anniversary dinners, and Holy Communion are events whose meanings far overshadow the food which is served at them. Each has its prescribed dress, rituals, and implicit or explicit assertion about the significance of what is being done. Thus man defines what it means to be human, orders his relationships with others, provides himself the assurance of continuity, and comforts himself with the knowledge that life has direction and meaning.

All of this is man's work; for it he takes credit and responsibility. He is in his own eyes a doer of great deeds, a hero wresting victory from the dark and treacherous forces which surround him, a singer remembering the myths of his destiny. He is man the master, "a little lower than the angels," a king in his own right.

The Gospel has no quarrel with these claims, nor does it disparage what man has made. For it sees the works of man as gifts which God gives in his care and love for his creatures. Man is indeed free and responsible to have dominion over the earth, to rule it in an orderly fashion, in justice and dignity.

EVERYMAN A KING

We are all kings—by divine appointment. As brothers by adoption of "great David's greater son," we possess a sovereign authority in the world. For every Christian is a free man, subject to no one, and he has God's mandate to serve as his liege man in caring for the creation.

To make such a sweeping assertion is to run the risk of a variety of misunderstandings, temptations, and perversions. The royal sovereignty of the Christian sounds very brave and exciting when forthrightly proclaimed from the pulpit. More accurately and more bitterly put, however, the tyranny of the saints has often been worse than the tyranny of sinners. For we have seen the godly in the seats of the mighty. There they have all too frequently shut out the truth, slammed the door of compassion on the defeated, and confiscated and destroyed the beautiful. They have blessed the heresy-hunters, absolved the enemies of justice, and bestowed accolades of wisdom on the prophets of organized ignorance.

All the hollering in the world will not change the record of history. Too often the pious have appeared on the scene after the battle has been won. In fact, upon occasion they have even claimed credit for the victory. As God's "picked representatives of the new humanity" they have been tempted to overrate the authority God has placed in their hands. The result of this overconfidence has sometimes led them to confuse responsible service with special privileges.

KINGDOMS IN COLLISION

The road to an understanding of the universal kingship of believers necessarily begins with a series of detours. Since the days when the Wise Men mistakenly went to the palace of Herod the King in Jerusalem, those who have been in search of the King of Kings have sought him out in the wrong places. Even when his appearance had about it something of the triumphal air of a royal procession, a close reading of the biblical account reveals a rather sorry spectacle. For surely that Palm Sunday march into Jerusalem must have looked like a bedraggled parade of misfits; a bearded prophet riding on an ass, accompanied by the rural rabble, a few rough fishermen from the Sea of Galilee, a hated tax-collector and collaborationist with Rome, beggars, prostitutes, possibly even a Samaritan or two, noisily shouting their way into a provincial capital. Hardly worth the notice of others who had seen Caesar and all his splendid legions march into Rome. Compared with that sight, this motley gang was certainly as unlikely a crew of candidates for the royal purple as one could imagine. In fact, except for the danger that in their enthusiasm they might run wild and create a public disturbance, this shouting pilgrimage of hallelujah-singers hardly merited attention. A Greek playwright and master of satire like Aristophanes might have written this scene as a biting caricature of the pretentions of certain pious stuffed shirts, "Behold, Jerusalem, thy king cometh unto thee, meek and lowly."

Palm Sunday indeed takes its meaning from the outrageous contrast with the elaborately staged triumphal entries of ancient kings. It speaks an everlasting No to every identification of the Kingdom of God with the kingdoms of this world, to every effort to establish the Kingdom out of the customary materials of the empire-builders of history—money, military might, the manipulation of power, diplomatic skill, treachery, bribery, betrayal, the exploitation of human weakness. Here the two kingdoms stand unalterably opposed to one another.

Two kingdoms in collision—but not quite; paradoxically and biblically stated, Yes and No. For they are both God's kingdoms; we belong to both. Not collision but entanglement, not confrontation but confusion, not clarity but obscurity describe the circumstances in which you and I and every man are caught. For the Kingdom of God in the life we know has no clear and fixed markers in space and time. Neither the organized church nor the Christian commonwealth, a community of saints-in-power whose royal chambers have been swept and cleared of all impurity, nor even some isolated colony of the faithful, protected from contamination by an iron curtain of ascetic discipline—none of these are the Kingdom, although the Kingdom may be found in all of them.

CHRISTIAN KINGSHIP: FREE, FAITHFUL, RESPONSIBLE

In brief, the kingdom of the redeemed may be present in every form of social organization in human society, but it must not be identified with any one form, neither holy church nor Christian commonwealth, nor must it be located in a pure, carefully restricted all-Christian ghetto of the righteous and the elect. Yet the kingdom must be embodied within the structures of life; to make it "purely spiritual," whatever that means, to have it float about freely in the air like the ghost of a bygone era, is to deprive it of all life and strength.

When does this kingdom have meaning for the individual Christian? Only when he understands that kingship means responsible service not sovereign authority, that freedom requires discipline, that the life of faith must be one of faith-full obedience.

To be a king is, therefore, to respond to the claim of the Word of God wherever I am, when it comes to me, in order that what God has given may be preserved and that men may live together in justice and dignity, in decency and freedom.

This response means that there is in Protestantism no room either for the clerical jack-of-all-trades, butting his nose into everyone's affairs as the community's Number One do-gooder, or for (an almost universal type) the devout occupant of the pew whose special stock in trade is "passing the buck" to someone else. The danger exists that Protestant laymen may become religious alibi artists of the first order, bargain-hunters in philanthropy, experts at the invocation of business reasons, reasons of state, friendship, local custom, and so forth for Christian inaction. While passing resolutions of concern, projecting into the future sentimental "programs" for uplifting the less fortunate, Christian laymen may run the risk of abdicating responsibility at the point where each man stands in his daily life. As Helmut Thielecke has said, "The road to hell is paved not merely with good intentions but with good reasons." [2]

Christian responsibility means that I must act where I am, breaking through the walls of accumulated injustice and age-old inertia to serve God's children. The persons most responsible for good housing for the poor, the unfortunate, the persons with the wrong color of skin or form of religious worship are the persons concerned with real estate in the community. No alibi for inaction will serve before God; here is where they see Christ naked, hungry, imprisoned, sick. This is their place of responsi-

[2] *The Waiting Father* (New York: Harpers, 1960), p. 166.

ble service. On the authority which God gives they must win their freedom from the entanglements of a perverted pattern of marketing—in God's name and for the sake of his creatures. Similarly the responsibility for integrity and decency in the mass media lies with merchants of ideas, the sponsors, network executives, publishers, and editors. The first responsibility for the production of goods serving the genuine needs of man belongs to the managers of the great industrial corporations. For example, George Romney, president of American Motors and a Mormon, pointed in the direction of the exercise of such responsibility when he broke through the recent jag of chrome-plated, overpowered, monstrously proportioned automobiles.

RESPONSIBLE SERVICE IN POLITICS

To be a free and sovereign Christian is, therefore, to be a responsible servant of the public good. No realm of community life, moreover, requires this service more than the realm of politics. Yet here again we must be careful not to assert the privilege of authority where we should seek the opportunity of service. Let it be plainly said that to serve responsibly within a community does not mean a Christian monopoly of public office, nor the introduction of public prayers into the ceremonies of government. By the grace of God men in public office in our land and elsewhere need not be Christians of any description to know right from wrong, to love justice and serve the common good. We need not invoke the theological half-truth that the good works of the heathen are sins in the sight of God. The good works of the heathen are good works; they are what God requires—what God makes possible. They do not merit salvation, and neither do mine nor yours nor any man's works.

A Christian's responsibility in political life expresses itself simply in the demand for justice. What my neighbor requires at this moment is my care and concern; just as I give my son food when he needs it, so I must use the treasures which God has given to serve the needs of others. But this is not enough. I must on the authority of faith, the authority of the Word, make the demand for justice the heart of my political action.

Here I make manifest the will of God in many ways. For my political activity helps to maintain the forms of human existence. This is what God requires of man. (I am not to hasten the end, impatient for Armageddon, for the end is in God's hands; he will see to it.) My task in public life is to strengthen whatever makes for improving the machinery of justice, for freedom, for bettering the condition of man.

The welfare state? Yes and No. Politically radical? Only by the perverse language of contemporary politics. Otherwise stated, the pre-eminent qualities of what the Christian asserts are the integrity of his concern for justice and the fidelity of his action to serve it. His political program is not to enact the Gospel into statute law—but in the most constructive way possible to stand for justice in all human relationships.

To be a Christian is also to be a free man, not bound to the authority of any other man, or to the authority of organizations, no matter what sanctity they may claim.

For to be a Christian is to be responsible before God and finally accountable only to him.

This statement is no assertion of anarchism or individualistic license. The Christian accepts the conditions of life in community, knowing that he must work with what is given in order to work in responsible freedom.

FREEDOM AND DISCIPLINE

Science offers the best illustration of this paradoxical combination of freedom and discipline. For science to be science must be free. It can brook no interference from the outside, whether the restraining hand claims patriotism, piety, orthodoxy, protection of the status quo, or any other virtue as its justification. This does not mean that science is either immoral or amoral. Its discipline flows from the nature of the tasks to be performed. The scientist stands in the service of truth and under its authority. His ultimate axiom is a Protestant one, namely that truth is better than goodness, no matter in what pious or attractive garb goodness may appear.

Truth furnishes the scientist with his authority and his discipline. For the rigor of scientific procedure, the never-ending re-examination of every conclusion, indeed the inbred skepticism with which all hypotheses, especially one's own, must be viewed, testify to a commitment of the most intense kind. Truth is the scientist's passion, and truth is his authority, come what may.

Yet, if he is a good scientist, he knows that truth itself is tentative, that all his descriptions are but a traveler's account of a passing scene, a landscape which no surveyor can ever map in any but provisional terms. In the language of the Christian, he realizes that all creation as we know it is transient, that its glory is but for a day, even the glory of the stars in their courses through the farthest heavens.

The tentative nature of truth suggests the hiddenness of the service of God in the life of science. This hiddenness may, furthermore, express itself in other ways. The scientist may be a man without explicit religious faith; he may even be hostile to organized religion as an enemy of the search for truth. He may find himself led to doubts and disillusionments of many kinds. These are the risks of his calling, taken in the full knowledge that his discoveries may drive him in one direction rather than another. The final conclusion is never in man's hands but God's; no matter whether he admits this or not, he must do his work as a free man.

This freedom must remain. For freedom is no longer freedom if we limit it to those who draw the same conclusions we do. We must judge the work of the scientist by the criteria of science—or we deny the validity of all he does. So long as he renders a true account of what he sees, he is a servant to the Creator, sometimes unconsciously and even against his will.

FAITHFUL SERVICE

What is true of the life of the scientist is true of the life of every other person. I must act freely, responsibly, faithfully wherever I am, neither worshiping nor disregarding what God has placed at my disposal. These are the instruments of his purpose. If I do not obey him within these conditions of my existence, where will I obey him?

I am consequently deeply involved in the life of my community at every point. Only through the faithful performance of the necessary tasks will the community survive.

Involvement, inescapably given as part of the creation, means responsible, free acceptance of the disciplines of work and faithful performance of every task.

This obedience does not mean a reactionary traditionalism. As the variety of human societies bears witness, alternative ways of earning a living, running a household, establishing and maintaining justice are available. To perpetuate the obsolete is unthinking conservatism. It is, in fact, usually a disguised defense of the past, often sentimental nostalgia combined with desperate adherence to inherited privilege.

Faithful service is constructive and imaginative, as ready to change when necessary as to protect what the past has bestowed. Its primary concern is with meeting the needs of all of God's creatures not with preserving the prerogatives of a few.

Faithfulness requires perseverance in the daily routines of life, tedious, tiring, and dirty though they may be. We are called to be faithful with our hands and pocketbooks, with our muscle and shoe leather, as well as with our tongues and our good intentions.

Faithfulness also requires competence. We must cultivate excellence, even when the task is not exciting. The cult of the amateur with its equalitarian assumption that every man is as good as his neighbor often leads to a false tolerance of sloppy workmanship, to an acceptance of a diversity of beliefs and programs on the assumption that it is sufficient to have sincerity, enthusiasm, and strongly-held convictions, no matter how obviously wrong-headed. But good intentions are no guarantee of performance. The faithful man is a competent man, and the price of competence is usually patient perseverance in learning how to become a master of the task assigned to him.

Nothing need here be said about a realistic awareness of one's limitations. This is not the issue. What is involved is the pious aversion to responsible action, the prudent ducking of the controversial for reasons of self-interest, friendship, business, or social involvement. Too many are willing to get on the record privately that, of course, they are in favor of decency and justice, peace or better human relations, but they refuse to be quoted. They reject the outright challenge to act. But the Christian man is accountable before God; neither reasons of state or of estate, fear of the anger of one's enemies or the disapproval of one's friends, will long hold before his questioning scrutiny of our motives. We are finally answerable only to Him.

THE CHRISTIAN'S AUTHORITY: THE WORD IN ITS FULNESS

So far nothing has been said about the authority of the Christian. But much has been implicit. First, the Christian himself stands under the mandate of God to be free, faithful, and responsible. Second, he finds the form of his service in the demand for justice. Areas of social concern are in the realm of the law; but the Christian serves them under the impetus of what the Gospel has done. Thus the Word in its fulness is the authority whose voice must be heard through his deeds.

The difference between the Christian and the non-Christian lies in the stand which the Christian takes as God's man. For the Christian no act is ever merely expedient, merely rational, or merely moral. Each act demonstrates the will of God. It carries a hidden divine dimension, often visible only to the eyes of faith. Faith gives each act a place in the whole picture, which adds height and depth to what is done.

Thus every Christian act has symbolic significance. Its full meaning is always part of a larger whole. In this sense we participate in the life of Christ, bearing one another's burdens, calling the defeated and the demoralized to the messianic banquet which the Father has prepared.

Yet we must admit that our generation sees the symbolism of the New Testament through unseeing eyes, even when the onlookers are conventionally religious. Dressed in the familiar garb of the Christian, we find it hard to be recognized as more than pious fanatics or interesting anachronisms. If we are to serve God as his liege men, ours will of necessity often be a hidden service, expressing itself in strange ways to an estranged generation.

We should not be surprised, therefore, to find the reenactment of our concerns in some of the secular myths that nightly fill our television screens. The biblical heroes may seem remote (except when sex and sin constitute a lower common denominator with our appetites), but each night on a scale which Homer could never have imagined the great legendary epics of our moral commitments are enacted for us. Perhaps we could not formulate their meanings precisely, but we often find ourselves deeply involved, even those of us who take the claim of the Gospel seriously. With Bret Maverick we are willing to bet our very lives on the turn of a single card, as though even here in the disguise of Chance "all things still work together for good." For we know that in each man's life a time may come when he must stand up and be counted, when he must wager all that he is, or he is less than a man. With Matt Dillon too we stride out into the disorderly night of our generation to vindicate justice, to rescue the weak, to restore courage to the defeated, self-respect to the failures.

"Gunsmoke" is indeed a kind of secular sermon on one dimension of the Christian life. It is in its way a parable of our kingship: faithfulness in one's assigned tasks, acceptance of suffering, contempt, hostility, even the risk of death in the performance of duty, and a constructive, creative, and imaginative application of the law in the midst of anarchy, on the frontier of existence, never taken in long by false respectability, never contemptuous of the publican and the sinner, sensing even in frustrated, angry, and desperate men and women some vestige of hope for the restoration of human dignity.

This is what it means to be a king—just precisely this kind of free obedience, faithfulness in drudgery and in danger, living without illusions of righteousness and in the constant hope of redemption, acting responsibly in the place where we find ourselves. To such a kingship we are called.

THE CHRISTIAN AS PROPHET IN LOVING PROTEST

"A news dispatch from India reports that a new prophet has arisen in the Ganges valley. The police are after him."

This brief anecdote, which I first heard from one of my professors many years ago and which I have since repeated to my students, no doubt defines the modern stereotype of the prophet.

THE CHRISTIAN: A MALADJUSTED PROPHET?

He is, of course, an agitator, a herald of the wrath of God upon an unjust generation, a pointer of the finger of condemnation at sinners public and private. He is, in addition, an eccentric sort of fellow, given to hearing voices and going into trances; he is unkempt, careless of the common courtesies, a bit of a lunatic in fact. Moreover, he can be positively dangerous to good order. He calls the established routines of life into question, attracts people away from their duties, discredits "the good people" and inspires visions of an apocalyptic future in the imaginations of the lazy; sometimes he even foments public disorder, at least indirectly.

No doubt he has some worthwhile things to say. Of course, there is some truth in his charges—but no one should expect the world to be perfect. Some people are going to cheat a little bit on their privileges. Leaders can't be expected to bear all the burdens of public affairs without some reward for what they are doing. A little corruption is a small price to pay for a quiet, well-ordered community. The worst forms of injustice will gradually be overcome, if only the confounded agitators would be patient.

Every Christian is expected to be a prophet. This is a hard fact, usually carefully obscured, neglected, and sometimes denied. But the difficulties the Christian encounters as a prophet have little to do with the stereotype. The prophet may, of course, be an agitator, stirring up the muddy channels of official action. He frequently has bad manners; telling the truth cannot always be a diplomatic act. He is obviously subversive of vested interests, often consciously and deliberately. He may also be, although not of necessity, personally eccentric, maladjusted, somewhat "crazy."

But in understanding the Christian man as a prophet and the necessity of prophesy, we had better put first things first. Then we can see how the prophet comes into being and what his proper work is.

When the great reformer, Martin Luther, wrote his famous treatise on Christian liberty in which he asserted both the universal priesthood and the universal kingship of the Christian man, he was playing the role of the prophet. Other reformers who wrote on Christian responsibility in the sixteenth century must certainly also be counted among the prophets. Yet paradoxically, Protestant theology does not generally include the prophet in this sense in its teachings about the forms of social order that exist in the creation nor does Protestant social ethics, with a few notable contemporary exceptions, have much to say about the prophetic responsibility of the ordinary Christian. What we teach about the world God made is, on the contrary, all too frequently used to anoint the existing social order with the holy oil of ecclesiastical benediction. We usually pay much more attention to the virtues of conformity and obedience. Injustice had best be endured; protest may lead to unrest, even to anarchy.

Properly speaking, the theologians are half-right. The prophet does not belong to the original creation. He is more correctly seen as the offspring of the Fall. It is his peculiar function to look upon the dark side of the created world, to see what man has made out of what God gave, the perversions and distortions, organized dishonesty, institutionalized brutality, systematic exploitation, the hate which brother bears to brother, the evil which nation plots against nation, the injustice which one race inflicts upon another. These the prophet is called to see, to measure against the infinite compassion of God and his everlasting love, and to announce that in these the very wrath of God will work itself out "unto the third and fourth generation."

PROTEST IN THE NAME OF TRUTH

The Christian man is no violent and wild-eyed anarchist. As priest and king he works to uphold what makes for an ordered and just world, caring for God's creation. But he knows the creation to be a fallen one.

He sees the stain of sin spread through the commonwealth, sees it infect home and school, workshop and playground, the halls of government and the sacred temples of the Most High. Driven both by his deep hurt at the violation of the mercy of God and by compassion for his fellows, he must speak out in protest.

His protest will be directed as much, nay more, at social injustice and corruption as it will be at individual immorality. Here especially he will encounter his gravest difficulties. There have always been those who were willing to launch out in the filth-ridden back alleys of the city of man to rescue individuals from the fires of hell. In fact, the energies of great moralists have been directed at the individual, urging him to personal piety, to self-denial and sacrifice, to the cultivation of the Christian virtues. Both the manuals of devotion and the hymnody of the church have abounded in this kind of moral effort. The realm of man's organized conduct of life has generally been overlooked. By artificial division of the realm of conduct into the private and the public, some Christians have on the one hand urged the serious searchers for religious truth to a cultivation of the inner life, often by a kind of implicit withdrawal from the more difficult public occupations, while on the other hand, condemning the world as corrupt beyond redemption, they have suggested that God wishes to keep the status quo just as it is. Thus they have sanctified the very order they have called depraved. Even more, they have suggested that in the fallen state of things a person has no choice in public life but to go along with the rules of the game as they are.

OBJECTION TO VIRTUE?

To determine whether this division of conduct into public and private exists let the reader but examine a few interesting paradoxes of the Christian life as lived in the mid-twentieth century. Here men can affirm, even in public, that they believe that in his personal relations the Christian should treat the Negro with all proper decency and kindness; they would not personally beat, kill, maim, or destroy the life or personality of another. At the same time, they defend as socially necessary a system of segregation which does precisely these things. While some do this with an uneasy conscience, there are those who publicly state that this dual ethic is in keeping with the Christian faith. (I am not even taking into account those Christians who would claim that such segregation is indeed the divine will and twist the Scriptures to their purpose.)

I am not, as some may suspect, suggesting that love is the cure for the ills of the social order. What has been said is directed against Christian abdication from the responsibility of working for justice in the social order; in the language of the previous chapter, I protest against the perversion of the royal authority of the Christian into a service of the status quo. In the world, love expresses itself in the demand for justice. Where the Christian sees injustice, he must speak out in prophetic protest. To do otherwise is to betray the will of God.

While the Christian accepts the existence of the family and state, for example, as manifestations of the providential love of God for his children, he must in obedience to the same God recognize perversion and corruption.

For the sake of the preservation of the created orders themselves, the Christian must speak out against institutionalized evil, against those who use what God gives to serve the ends of tyranny, exploitation, rapine, and murder. When men write injustice into law, when they use what God has given to all to enrich themselves, to subject others to their service, to deny opportunities for decent human existence to men on account of color, race, creed, or any other such irrelevant consideration, the Christian must cry out in God's name. When business firms, for example, "accept the resignation" of an employee because he has stood for social justice and decency in housing, when we are told that obedience to what law, morality, and justice alike demand may be bad for business, then the Christian may ask by what right any business firm or other organization which forces justice to serve its private ends can set itself up as a judge of moral conduct.

For everything that is here asserted the prophets of the Old Testament offer overwhelming support. They saw sin in its collective form as well as in its individual embodiment. They announced the wrath of God upon the marauding imperialists and ravaging monsters of their day. Equal support is found in the New Testament, for it sees both established religion and imperial government collaborate in striking down the man of Nazareth. In the terrible visions of the Apocalypse, the enemy is Babylon, the persecuting empire itself, not just an aggregate of malicious individual persons.

Skeptics might also take note of the precedent of the Reformation. Luther, Calvin, and the other reformers attacked the institutionalized corruption of the church.

A bad bishop is an evil that can be endured; the organized ecclesiastical corruption of Christian authority in the papacy must be confronted and condemned.

The prophetic awareness of sin in the radical Protestant analysis of human existence goes one step further. For it sees that the systematic perversion of what God gives can occur within the very patterns of obedience which God has offered to his children. All of us are priests—yet the record of the last four centuries shows a persistent and continuing perversion of the doctrine of the universal priesthood. In chapter two we touched upon certain elements of this perversion. Here we may pursue the matter a little further.

PROTESTANTISM'S DANGER

The great danger from which Protestantism suffers and to which time and time again it has succumbed is to make the priesthood the monopoly of the clergy. The Protestant refusal, generally speaking, to employ the term "priest" for the one set aside for the office of the ministry may itself reflect an awareness that priest and minister are not the same thing. All of us are priests. The minister is one called to an office with particular duties in the community of the faithful. Yet over and over the priesthood has in fact become the special property of a professional class, who then are expected to do what they cannot do, namely to be religious for the rest of us, not only to be learned in the Word of God on our behalf but to perform our Christian duties. For example, the primary responsibility for breaking the pattern of injustice in housing does not lie with the clergy, nor with the professors of social ethics or social science, lay or religious. The primary responsibility lies with the builders, subdividers, and those concerned with real estate. God has put them there to seek justice and be merciful. To allow the clergy to usurp this role, even to foist it upon them—as something one can expect from one who is to be professionally pious but not practical—is a denial of the universal priesthood. To affirm the universal priesthood those who have responsibility in a given situation must assume it without shifting it to others.

A related corruption of the priesthood is found in radical laicism and extreme congregationalism. The office of the ministry is a distinct office within the church. To make the minister's duties the creatures of a majority vote, to substitute submission to the will of the congregation for the vow to proclaim the truth of God's Word, to threaten the livelihood of the minister if his preaching touches on unpleasant sins near home (in particular social sins) is to claim for the universal priesthood an authority over the proclamation of the Gospel which was never given to it.

Equally perverted is the reduction of the Christian life to ritualism and priestly routine. To follow certain forms of worship as an expression of the continuity of the fellowship of the saints through all generations is one matter; to sanctify tradition, to validate liturgical forms on the basis of antiquity, to standardize worship within a few major rubrics may lead to priestcraft and idolatry of ecclesiastical custom. The Christian as a prophet must always keep a sharp eye on the Christian as priest, for sin, like charity, tends to begin at home.

AGAINST OR FOR THE CHURCH?

In a like manner the Christian as prophet must keep an eye on the Christian as king. For the abuse of power is not limited to the ungodly. Righteousness has more than once been an excuse for tyranny and persecution. The history of the Christian church is indeed cluttered up with more than a small share of the mementoes of the abuse of power in the name of God. This recorded history is a warning to Christians at all times to be on guard against the misuse of power by the church.

Quite obviously, then, the first word of the prophet must always be the word against the church. It is a small wonder, therefore, that priests and ecclesiastical princes have rarely felt any strong affection for the prophet. For the prophet is one sent to speak for the freedom of man to serve God, to protest against every abuse of freedom, whether by religious or by secular autocrats.

The first place in which man must be free to serve God is in the church. Man must be free both to take his place within the fellowship of believers and within that fellowship to serve God without restraint or dictation. Every Christian must be free to do so. My neighbor cannot believe for me, nor can my pastor, nor an ascetic kneeling on a corncob pallet, not even the Holy Father in Rome. Every man must do his own believing; he must protest against whatever prevents his faith from an honest and healthy fruition.

This means that every Christian—not just the minister—must protest against every restriction placed on the fellowship of the Gospel. To set any other conditions for membership in the church than those which Christ himself set is to pervert the household of faith. To protest this perversion is as much the responsibility of the pew as it is of the pulpit. All of us are prophets.

But the prophet cannot stop with the word against the church. To do so would be to misconstrue his prophetic role. For he speaks the word in the church in order that in and through the church the prophetic word may also be spoken in the world. Except in unusual circumstances, furthermore, he speaks from within the church. For voluntarily to separate one's self from the household of faith, as long as freedom remains to witness to the Word of God, is altogether too often a matter of spiritual pride, of a judgment of spiritual superiority. When the Christian speaks within the church, he speaks to himself and brings himself under his own judgment. This is as it should be. When he speaks from outside the church, or from within a new fellowship, from within his own peculiar circle of disciples, he too easily passes lightly over his own shortcomings.

In and through the church the prophet may speak to the priest and king, not only in their explicit roles (their Sunday morning religious practices), but also and particularly to their hidden and pervasive participation in the world. He calls the Christian to the daily exercise of reverence and intercession, to the daily exercise of freedom, faithfulness, and responsibility. He must keep the conscience of the Christian fellowship sharp.

PROTEST OUT OF LOVE

But he must do more. He must also speak a prophetic word to those outside the fellowship. Here his word derives in a peculiar sense from the law, for though he speaks on behalf of the freedom of the Gospel, though he speaks on behalf of the freedom and integrity of man, his word is heard as a word of condemnation. To the man who does not believe, the Gospel is not Gospel but law. The word of love spoken on behalf of the oppressed sounds like folly to the unbeliever; rejecting it, he brings himself under judgment, for he claims righteousness for his way of life. For example, the word of love spoken on behalf of peace and reconciliation among the nations arouses in many who hear it only anger, resentment, bitterness, legal prosecution, and retaliation. By claiming righteousness for what they do, even in the name of the Gospel, they who are irritated make their own actions the basis of their judgment.

The prophet must, of course, accept the same consequences. He cannot claim exemption. He may only witness to what the Spirit compels him to say, humbly and openly, neither in anger against his protagonist, nor with an air of moral superiority. He must, moreover, accept without condition the Christian witness of those who disagree with him. The rightness or wrongness of a particular program of political action on behalf of peace is not the issue—about this both sides may be wrong; of this they are not the ultimate judges. The question is whether or not in the proclamation of his inner conviction the prophet breaks fellowship with the other man, whether one or the other now presumes to stand before God as "more righteous" than this miserable publican.

The tendency to place a high premium on the respectability of the church and its members poses a special problem. Respectability as such need not be a hindrance to the prophet's demand for justice. But when respectability prevents the members of a congregation or a church from discharging their responsibility to all segments of society, it assumes an exclusive character not in harmony with justice or love. By restricting themselves to caring for those in a certain social bracket they cling to little privileges they have gained. This substitution of privilege for responsibility calls for protest and correction.

It is a matter of record that the word of the prophet has most often been directed against those for whom being devout is synonymous with a certain level of social standing. This is not to say that they are bad people. We malign the Pharisees, the particular antagonists of our Lord, if we see them as consciously hypocritical, deliberate exploiters of religion for the sake of power, or as evil men using the cover of goodness to carry out nefarious schemes of political and social intrigue. Quite the contrary, they were for the most part serious students of the Scriptures, engaged in a rigorous discipline of the self for the glory of God, given beyond their contemporaries to works of charity. Even the Pharisee in the famous parable did not claim credit for his own righteousness; he thanked God—just as devout Christians in our day may give God thanks for preserving them in the paths of morality and decency.

Still, the word of the prophet must be the word against these people. For by their very respectability, they may close the fellowship to those who hunger desperately for help. If the yardstick they use is scaled to human achievement, then it becomes so easy for the devout to identify themselves with the elect and to include the publicans and sinners among the eternally damned.

To do this is to forget the demands of the Word. Before God no human yardstick is adequate. The myth of the celestial account book is not just a bit of pious invention; in the form in which it is usually recounted it is a fraud. Before God all our righteousness is as filthy rags. The point of the parable of the last judgment is not to remind us to perform the seven works of mercy; it asks whether or not we have looked into the eyes of the man farthest down and there seen the Christ. This is the crucial question. This is the message of the prophet, that we may see the Christ in the downtrodden and the forgotten, in the demoralized and the abandoned.

No man is therefore beyond redemption. Every man is intended by the grace of God for freedom, for faithfulness, for responsibility. Whenever and wherever the community of the faithful forgets this or government, business, school, or anything else perverts and obstructs, the prophet must speak out forthrightly and loudly.

The greatest danger lies not so much, however, in the deliberate denial of this universal concern as it does in the persistence of practices which in actuality obstruct its realization. Quite often, too, these practices have the sanctity of pious concern and the authority of love. Yet they sentimentalize love and they perpetuate injustice. No clearer example may be found than in some of the continuing practices of organized charity, private and public, inside and outside the church. Any practice of charity which is an act of condescension, of doing good to "lesser breeds without the law" is a perversion of the Gospel. To offer baskets at Christmas while ignoring or opposing the forms of public action that would deal with the roots of poverty is misguided benevolence at best and cynical abuse of possessions at its worst. To use organized private charity as a means to power and prestige in the community, as a means of having one's own way—to prevent the extension or improvement of public welfare, for example—is as much a sin as picking the pockets of the poor. To oppose public action to improve housing or health, while refusing to implement any effective private alternative, is to take the name of God in vain, even if it be done in the name of freedom. This is a much worse blasphemy than the verbal invectives of the ungodly and the ignorant.

THE PROPHET SPEAKS AGAINST HIMSELF

But it must be remembered that the prophet is as much a sinner as the one he challenges. This fact he dare never forget. The hard, unloving reputation of the moral fanatic is well known from the chronicles of human history. The Christian prophet is no moralist in the usual sense. Yet because he is concerned particularly with the abuse of freedom, he easily becomes the victim of his own moral enthusiasms. If he possesses the gift of rhetoric, he may fall under his own spell. Rigorous self-examination is a daily requirement in his life. The word of the prophet must always be spoken first of all to the prophet himself.

The Christian as prophet finds his role most quickly, yet also in its most difficult form, in the place of his daily employment. Prophesy is no Sunday morning luxury. As a teacher, for example, my place of primary responsibility is the academic community. This does not mean that my first word must be directed against the college president. It may well be that the demand for the freedom of the mind from outworn intellectual slogans, from stifling of the mind of the student in the regimented routine of organized pedantry, from the abuse of the arbitrary tyranny of the classroom—must first of all be a word against myself and my colleagues. I may then also be driven to make the same demand of those in higher places of authority; in private at least most professors have little trouble with this role. Finally, I may need to confront the student, too. Here I am least likely to overlook my obligations because I am tempted to assume an air of intellectual superiority.

What is true of the professor is true in every other occupation; each of us is called to be a prophet. It is, of course, always easier to sweep before another man's door. Again, I repeat, the cry against injustice in the economic order ought to come first from the business community itself; the protest against the abuse of medical practice from the physicians. What we too often get instead are long-winded exercises in self-glorification and self-defense.

But let us return to sweeping in front of our own doors. If the professor wishes to be a prophet—God knows if he has integrity he cannot be anything else—he should be willing to accept the consequences. A recent study of the threats to freedom during the era of the late Senator McCarthy of Wisconsin [1] revealed that many

[1] Neither on grounds of patriotism nor of anti-Communism was there ever any basis for tolerating this travesty upon democratic institutions except timidity in high places.

professors felt their academic freedom threatened. Some were actually threatened. But these threats were no excuse for the pitiful weeping and wailing in the groves of academe. If professors want to discuss controversial subjects, as in all honesty they must, they cannot expect to be matinee idols. Freedom is a hard-bought thing; the price of it may include public abuse, private slander, and the opposition of protectors of the status quo. Any fool ought to know this. If he wants to be the spokesman of unpopular causes, he should not expect others to treat them as popular.

This does not mean that I am in favor of the continuation of abuse, slander, or organized pressure. Not in the least. But I suspect that one of the worst enemies of academic freedom during the McCarthy episode was scholarly timidity itself. To paraphase Luther, the way to fight the devil is to tell him to go to hell in plain English. A little professional courage along with some political courage might have saved the country from some of the worst displays of demagogic excess.

God has set each one of us in his place within his creation. In this place, as God's picked representatives of the new humanity, we are to make his Word manifest in priestly care and intercessory action, through royal freedom, faithfulness and service, and by prophetic protest against injustice and on behalf of the dignity and integrity of man. For some of us one role will be more important than the other, but we are called to each of them. As occasion warrants, we must not shrink from the performance of our appointed tasks.

All of us are priests, kings, and prophets. Let us therefore live life with a due sense of our high calling, knowing what God has done for us in our rebirth through Christ. God be merciful to us in our shortcomings and strengthen us by his Spirit to ever-renewed conformity to the mind of Christ.

Type used in this book
Body, 10 on 13 Caledonia
Display, Times Roman
Paper: Spring Grove Antique "R"